Teaching
With

"Impatience is a frequent problem with children and adolescents that is often overlooked in this day of ADHD overdiagnosis. In *Teaching Children Patience Without Losing Yours*, Dr. Jerry Wilde and Polly Wilde have written a sensible explanation of the symptoms and effects of low frustration tolerance. Using Rational-Emotive techniques, parents are guided through a practical training procedure to improve their child's patience. I highly recommend this book."

Carol DeLucia, LCSW
Diplomate in Clinical Social Work
Certified Behavioral-Cognitive Therapist

"*Teaching Children Patience Without Losing Yours* captures the importance of a seemingly foregone yet vital skill for our childrens' future. The Wildes present helpful approaches and techniques, based on sound research, to help all parents instill patience in their children. Moreover, this book is a fresh and timely reminder to us that patience is in our control and can contribute to a higher quality of life."

Dr. Russell A. Sabella
Assistant Professor of Counselor Education
Department of Educational & Counseling Psychology
University of Louisville

Teaching Children Patience

Without Losing Yours

Teaching Children Patience *Without Losing Yours*

Jerry Wilde, Ph.D.
Polly Wilde

LGR Publishing
3219 N.W. C St.
Richmond, IN 47374

LGR Publishing
3219 N. W. C St.
Richmond, IN 47374

Teaching Children Patience

For information: LGR Publishing
(800) 369 - 5611

Printing History
First Printing 1999

ISBN : 0 - 9657610 - 2 - 9

PRINTED IN THE UNITED STATES OF AMERICA
10 9 8 7 6 5 4 3 2 1

Acknowledgments

The authors would like to thank the many individuals who assisted them in the preparation of this book.

To our children (Anna and Jack)...you're the first thing we hear when we wake in the morning (thanks, Jack) and the last thing we think about when we go to sleep. Thank you for helping us laugh more, live more and love more. Mom and Dad love you very, very much.

To our parents, who taught us the hard lessons about patience so that we might pass them along to our children, thanks for all your support.

Many individuals read early versions of this manuscript and their input greatly improved this book. Special recognition for service "above and beyond the call of duty" goes to James Larson, Robert F. Chapman, Russell A. Sabella, Jerry Wyett and Carol DeLucia. Thank you all for your time and energy.

To the mothers, fathers, teachers, counselors and other individuals who touch the lives of children...never give up. You have the most important jobs in the world.

Other books by Jerry Wilde

Hot Stuff to Help Kids Chill Out: The Anger Management Book

Why Kids Struggle in School: A Guide to Overcoming Underachievement

Treating Anger, Anxiety and Depression in Children and Adolescents: A Cognitive-Behavioral Perspective

Anger Management in Schools: Alternatives to Student Violence

Rational Counseling with School-Aged Populations: A Practical Guide

Rising Above: A Guide to Overcoming Obstacles and Finding Happiness

The Subject is Joy: A Path to Lifetime Contentment Through Value-Based Living (with John Wilde)

Contents

1

If at first you don't
succeed you're running
about average.
M.H. Alderson

Introduction

We live in a fast-paced society that celebrates excess. Corporate America encourages us to want more, buy more, and have more of everything. At the same time, the advertising that continuously bombards us carries the message that life and happiness can be quick and easy.

So as you warm up your lunch in your microwave, then sit in your easy chair with your remote control and instant coffee, think about the things in life that matter most, such as family, friendships, health, and education. These things cannot be purchased or maintained without some hard work and patience. This book is about patience and how to help our children learn the art and value of delaying gratification.

Despite what you may have heard, patience is more

than just a virtue. It is a key component to success in most of the truly important things in life. It needs to be taught, developed, and nurtured through years of life experience. As the saying goes, "Few things worth having come easily."

Therefore, helping kids develop the ability to be patient is one of the most important and useful lessons we can teach them. Developing patience in children takes continuous and consistent effort. It can't happen without parents and caregivers who are willing to examine their own habits as role models for patience.

Patience and Parental Interaction

According to Harvard University economist Victor Fuchs, children have lost between ten and twelve hours of parental time per week since 1960.1 If this loss is projected from birth until the age of majority, it totals 11,232 hours less parental time children receive in this generation than those children born in 1960! That comes to 468 days, 15.6 months or 1.3 years less than kids of the 1960s received from their parents. Add to this the fact that growing up certainly hasn't gotten any easier in the past 35 years, and the loss of time children spend with parents is further magnified.

Some of the "thirtysomething" crowd may remember being told in grade school they would have to learn what to do with their leisure time when they got older. In 1967, in testimony to a Senate subcommittee, a well-known economist predicted that by 1985 people would be working only 22 hours a week or they would be able to retire by the age of 38.2 It was also believed that numerous time-saving devices would produce a glut of leisure time. Your authors would like to suggest a blue ribbon panel be appointed to determine who was responsible for this nonsense and punish these individuals accordingly. A fitting consequence would be to require these people to take turns doing the banking, shopping, and all the other tasks that seem to eat away at our leisure time for those of us who feel "glutless."

Cultural Warp Speed and Kids

What effect does this lack of time have on children? As you might have guessed, the effect is not positive. It would be inaccurate and too convenient to say a lack of parental time has "caused" specific childhood problems. However, there can be no question that parents' involvement with their kids has a powerful influence. Parental involvement relates to a number of important outcomes. What follows are a few of the ways in which lack of parental time has negatively affected our children.

Patience and Academic Difficulties

The news from the educational front is encouraging but there is still plenty of room for improvement. It's difficult to pick up a newspaper or magazine today without seeing an article about education and what can be done to help students be more successful. American students have some of the lowest levels of achievement of any developed nation.

In a recent study by the International Association for the Evaluation of Educational Achievement, American high school students came in seventh out of ten countries in physics, ninth out of ten in chemistry, and dead last in mathematics. American ninth graders tied with Singapore and Thailand for fourteenth place in science.3

These findings are somewhat deceiving and can partly be explained by the ways other countries report data collected from their students. America is the only country that reports scores from **all** students.

While this may explain why American students do not measure up to international standards, it does not explain why our students' scores have been dropping in comparison to measures obtained from earlier generations of Americans. There has been a steady decline in academic achievement over the past thirty years. Across the nation, combined Scholastic Aptitude Test (SAT) scores have fallen 70 points since 1963. While there have been slight increases, achievement levels are still far below the benchmarks set by classes of previous American students.

Could it be that today's kids are not as bright as other generations? Actually, the opposite is true. Today's students are actually scoring higher on intelligence tests than earlier generations. The reason for the decline in our educational performance may have more to do with the decline of families and the dominance of values that are in conflict with education. As our society decays, so do the individual institutions that make up that society.

American students spend more time watching television and less time doing homework than kids in any other developed country. Does anyone think these two factors are unrelated?

Staring at the television is easy. All you need is a screen and a thumb to work the remote control. Doing homework takes sacrifice today for a payoff later. That's another way of saying it requires patience. Children will learn how to have fun; it is up to their parents to help them acquire patience and self-discipline.

Patience and Problems with Depression

Depression in America has been increasing with each passing generation since records were kept around the turn of the century. Some researchers have reported the increase in depression as "nearing epidemic proportions." The number of teenagers admitted to private psychiatric hospitals has increased fifteen fold since 1971, even though the adolescent population has shrunk over the past twenty-five years.[4]

While depression has probably always been part of the human condition, it was much less common during the earlier years of this century. People born around 1925 had very low rates of depression. Only 4% had suffered a bout of depression during their lifetime. When examining data from individuals born before World War I, only 1% had been depressed. In contrast, people born around 1955, who had obviously not lived nearly as long as those born in the 1920s, were already much more likely to have suffered from depression. Nearly 7% had been diagnosed as depressed by their early twenties.[5]

Perhaps most distressing was the finding by the Centers for Disease Control in a survey of over 11,000 students in all fifty states. Twenty-seven percent (27%) of those surveyed said they had seriously thought about attempting suicide.[6]

I (JW) discovered alarming results during my own research into adolescent depression. For instance, a commonly used questionnaire, the Beck Depression Inventory (BDI), was administered to 80 high school students from a small midwestern town. Twenty-five scored in a range that would indicate the presence of at least mild depression. The results of this study indicated that almost one out of three (31%) of the students responded that they at times felt mildly to moderately depressed.[7]

What has changed during the course of this century? While there are biochemical causes of depression, the human brain has certainly not changed substantially in the past 90 years. The cause of this epidemic of depression has more to do with people's beliefs and attitudes. Children are raised to think they should possess everything their hearts' desire. When things don't come easily, kids take it as a sign that either a) the world is a terrible, unfair place; b) the future is hopeless or c) they are somehow lacking and deserve to suffer. Attitudes, not events, are responsible for most depression. If children and adolescents believe one or all of the above ideas, how could they feel anything but depressed?

Patience and Drug Use

There is an association between parental involvement and adolescent drug use. The more involved parents are in the lives of their kids, the less likely the adolescents are to engage in drug and alcohol use.

Similar to news on American education, drug and alcohol use is declining but the rates are still alarming. As frightening as the thought of substance abuse may be, it had better be considered a potential in any adolescent's life.

Consider the findings from the "Monitoring the Future" study, a series of annual surveys of some 50,000 students in over 400 public and private secondary schools in the nation.

In 1995, marijuana use continued the strong resurgence that began in the early nineties. Among eighth graders, the percentage of students reporting use in the previous 12 months has risen 250% since 1991 (i.e., from 6% in 1991 to 16% in 1995). Among 10th graders, the annual prevalence has nearly doubled from 15% in 1992 to 29% in 1995. Among 12th graders, the annual prevalence has increased by more than half from 22% in 1992 to 35% in 1995. Nearly five percent of today's high school seniors use marijuana daily.

The proportions reporting any LSD use in the previous 12 months were 3%, 7% and 8% respectively for eighth, 10th and 12th graders, respectively. The annual prevalence rates for use of cocaine in any form are 2.6%, 3.5%, and 4% for grades eight, 10 and 12, respectively.

Beliefs about how harmful various drugs are have proven to be important determinants of use. There was a sharp decline in the perceived risk of marijuana use at all three grade levels. For example, while 79% of 12th graders in 1991 thought that regular marijuana users run a "great risk" of harming themselves physically or in other ways, by 1995 only 61% of 12th graders felt that way.8

You may be thinking, "What is the relationship between drug use and patience?" Good question. Here's the connection: Feeling "good" through drug use is instantaneous. The satisfaction that comes through worthwhile pursuits takes hard work and patience. Drug use is a temporary escape from life whereas hard work and patience are an investment in the future.

The Need for Just Such a Book

This book can be used by any adults who are interested in helping children learn the self-discipline it takes to be patient. It is not a book written specifically for parents of children with attention-deficit hyperactivity disorder (ADHD), but certainly many of the ideas contained within these pages will be applicable. Like all important lessons we teach our children, we may be reminded of a few important points ourselves.

We decided to write this book to give parents a hand in the most difficult job around (parenting). Who are we and why are we the people to write this book?

First, we want you to know **we are parents**. Nothing annoys us more than people telling us how to do something they've never done themselves. We've been "in the trenches" with parents everywhere—walking the floor in the middle of the night with a sick baby, withstanding temper tantrums, and coaxing a child to eat "two more bites of peas."

Our daughter, Anna, is four at the time of this writing. She is an everyday, normal, happy, and healthy little girl who loves coloring, swinging, ice cream cones, and bike rides. We didn't realize what an easy baby she was until after having our second child.

Then along came our son, Jack. He's an adorable beast. It's a good thing he's cute because he sure is a lot of work. Though probably much like most kids, compared with Anna, Jack is much more challenging.

When we had Anna, we had a feeling many people were disappointed because she was such an easy baby. We suspected they had been hoping and praying we'd have a "challenging baby" so we could empathize with them regarding their trials and tribulations with their kids.

I (JW) have been working as a child psychologist for ten years. During the day I work in a school, and a couple of evenings a week I work with a local counseling agency where I specialize in child and family counseling.

I (PW) am educated as, and have worked as, a math teacher. However, for the past four years I have worked as a freelance reporter for our local newspaper. The work allows great flexibility so that I can stay at home with Anna and Jack.

Please forgive us if it's too obvious we love our kids to death. We will use little vignettes from our family to illustrate certain points, but we'll try not to over do it. We do not want to appear to be "the perfect parents" because we are not! We do spend an awful lot of time with Anna, Jack and all the kids in our neighborhood. We have spent virtually all of our adult lives studying, treating, and playing with children. To this day, we're still most comfortable being around kids. If we had to make a choice between a kick ball game and a cocktail party, it wouldn't be a tough decision. Kids are just so unpretentious and that's a rare commodity today.

We're real parents with real kids trying hard to pass on a few of the lessons we've learned through our personal and professional experiences. We hope you enjoy the book and learn some important skills.

Getting Started

Make no mistake about it, patience is learned. Kids don't like taking turns. They don't like waiting. They don't like sharing with a brother or sister. And why should they? None of the above-mentioned situations (taking turns, waiting, and sharing) benefit them directly.

Kids do not come by these cooperative behaviors naturally. They must be taught. Unlike simple addition, patience is a quality that cannot be learned in a single lesson. It is a seed that must be sown early and nurtured throughout a child's formative years. Practicing and learning to be patient is a never-ending process. Happily, the fruits of your labor will be well worth the effort.

When to Start?

Start teaching patience early. Like most things in life, it is much easier to learn when young. Unfortunately, too many parents realize they have a problem after 15 years of indulging their child's every whim and fancy. It is very hard to change behavior after it has been practiced and reinforced for 15 years. Once the genie is out of the bottle, it's difficult to get it back in.

So start from age 0. Of course you can't teach a baby much of anything directly, but you can reward patient behavior and ignore as much whining as is humanly possible.

Also, from a very early age parents can present choices that reward patience. Such patterns, if used consistently, do have a lasting impact on a child's personality. For example, you can allow a child a short

10

time to play after school or a longer time if the child delays gratification and does his or her homework first and plays afterward. Having a mindset for patience will allow you to come up with these choices easily and consistently.

Feeding Time

One of the things we've done with our children once they are eating baby food is to feed them slowly while the entire family eats. Lots of parents feed the baby first so they can sit down and have a nice dinner. But we found that an uninterrupted dinner with small children is impossible unless they are asleep.

So why not feed the child slowly while you eat, taking time between bites so the child has to wait? We have done this with our kids and it works quite well. We're sending them the message, "Yes, your needs will be attended to. You won't go hungry, but you have to wait just like the rest of us." It's little things like this that make up the lessons of patience.

Bathroom Time

Our daughter is like most kids and doesn't like washing her hands every time she goes to the bathroom, though she's turned hand washing into a pretty consistent habit (with a lot of coaxing and reminding). It's hardest for her to remain consistent when we're doing something fun and she doesn't want to miss any of the action. There are times that the parental role modeling of delaying gratification is very important. Consistently engaging in these behaviors eventually produces habits and that lays the ground work for the difficult hurdles that will follow.

Overview

What follows is an examination of patience and why it is important. We'll present some of the fascinating research on the correlations between a child's ability to delay gratification (i.e., be patient) and outcomes much later in life.

Next we'll examine characteristics of the impatient child. What type of problems do they experience and what can be done to help them?

Can patience be taught? We believe it can and there is increasing evidence that kids can and do learn specific techniques to increase patience. Activities that teach patience will be presented.

Impatient children typically have difficulties coping with frustration and anger. A detailed analysis of anger management will be offered. Suggestions for improving academic performance will also be addressed.

If you are the parent of an impatient child, keep in mind this problem did not come about quickly and will not disappear overnight. One of the most important things you can do is prepare yourself for the long haul. Said another way, one of the most important traits *you* can display is patience. If you want your child to learn patience, start by being patient. There are no short cuts here, but as we said earlier, the rewards are worth every ounce of effort.

2

Dear God,
I pray for patience.
And I want it <u>right</u> <u>now</u>!
Oren Arnold

Why is Patience Important?

What do kids need to live happy, robust, and
fulfilling lives? They need healthy food in order to get the
nutrition necessary for their growing bodies and minds.
They need shelter. Of course, needs such as food and
shelter are fundamental. It's also a good idea if someone
makes certain they don't play in the streets or eat cat food.
Thankfully, very few parents need to have "survival" as
their primary goal for their children. So assuming kids are
healthy physically, what else do they need?

Children turn out best when the adults in their lives
put the kids' needs first. When you think about it, that's a

pretty good description of quality parenting—putting your kids' needs in front of your own. It's difficult at times, but whoever said parenting would be easy? Parenting is not for wimps.

If parents love their kids desperately, and most do, they want more for their children than "adequate." Parents want their children to have extraordinary lives filled with diplomas, scholastic and athletic achievements, and challenging careers. If you're one of *those* parents, you need to understand why patience is so important to attain the good things in life. **The ability to delay gratification (i.e., be patient) is one of the best predictors of success in life.** Don't trust us on mere faith alone. Let's examine the research on delayed gratification.

The Marshmallow Studies

A psychologist named Walter Mischel has conducted a series of experiments that test childrens' ability to delay gratification. Mischel and his colleagues at Stanford University started the procedures by letting children examine some toys. The children were told the toys could be played with later. Next, the experimenter taught the children a game in which the experimenter left the room. The child was told the experimenter would come back immediately if a bell was rung. Each child was then shown a pair of treats which differed in value (for example, one versus two marshmallows).

The child was then told he or she must wait until the experimenter returned to the room to attain the treat he or she most desired (i.e., two marshmallows). If the child couldn't wait, the bell could be rung at any time and he or she would receive the less desired treat (i.e., one marshmallow). After the experimenter was certain the child understood the rules, the youngster was left alone in the room and observed through a two-way mirror.

Keep in mind there were many variations to this basic experiment and the researchers were interested in a lot of factors other than just how long the children would wait. The researchers wanted to determine if the ability to delay gratification at a young age (i.e., preschool) could predict success in later life.

The Findings

More than 600 preschoolers were tested during the initial portion of these experiments. Ten years following the marshmallow studies, the researchers again contacted the families. The adolescents who were able to wait longer (when they were tested as preschoolers) were described by their parents as:

1) More academically competent
2) More socially competent
3) Better at coping with frustration
4) More able to resist temptation
5) More able to cope with stress
6) More verbally fluent
7) More attentive
8) Better planners
9) More able to think ahead
10) More mature1

Look once again at the above descriptors and realize it is a virtual laundry list of positive characteristics in adolescents. The ability to delay gratification (i.e., patience) will serve your children quite well.

Preschoolers vs. Elementary

Why is it so hard for children to delay gratification? One of the answers seems to be "because they don't know how to make waiting easier." In another experiment, 272 preschoolers and 48 first to third graders were shown either a) real rewards (marshmallows), b) picture versions of the rewards, or c) irrelevant objects while they waited. *The preschoolers actually preferred to view the real rewards (marshmallows) while they waited.* The older children did not choose the marshmallows, indicating an important difference between the preschoolers and elementary students. The older children knew how to make waiting less frustrating.[2] Older children seemed to understand that looking at real marshmallows would make waiting much more difficult.

Kids learn the basic "rules" about waiting for rewards as they get older. As mentioned above, most third graders understand it is easier to wait if the rewards are not in sight. By sixth grade most kids understand it will be easier to wait if you think distracting thoughts rather than focus on eating the marshmallow. Once again, preschoolers do not have these insights. This goes a long way toward explaining their difficulties delaying gratification.[3]

The Role of Distraction

Mischel and his colleagues have been interested in the effect distraction would have on children's ability to delay gratification. They allowed children to distract themselves from the reward by either a) playing with toys or b) thinking "fun" thoughts. A third group of children was not given toys or instructed to think "fun" thoughts.

Children using some type of distraction (toys or "fun" thoughts) waited significantly longer than the third group that was not given any help occupying their minds. It is important to note that only certain types of thoughts lead to longer waiting times. Thinking "sad" thoughts led to short delay times, as did thinking about the rewards themselves.4

Another experiment with 90 preschoolers had the kids look at slides while they waited. The slides were either of a) images of their treats, b) other treats, or c) a blank screen. Additionally, some of the children were instructed to think about their treats, for this experiment, pretzels. Kids were told,

> "You can think about how salty the
> pretzels are. Pretzels are really
> salty. Think about how salty the
> pretzels are in your mouth. Pretzels
> are crunchy, too. Think about how
> crunchy the pretzels are when you
> chew on them."

Other children were told to think about mints and graham crackers, but these were not the treats they were going to receive.

Mischel and his colleagues found that kids looking at the image of their treat could wait longer than the children looking at the irrelevant image or the blank screen. However, the most important factor was the children's thoughts during the wait. When instructed to think about the qualities of their treat (i.e., the pretzel) they had significantly shorter delay times.5

Reasoning and Patience

It may come as a surprise to some adults, but research suggests that preschoolers do respond to reason. Let us explain.

Kindergartners were asked to choose between a small but immediate reward (one candy bar today) or a larger reward they would have to wait for (two candy bars tomorrow). No matter which option they selected, the children were then told about another student who had made the opposite choice from their own and asked to give reasons he or she had selected the other reward. When children who had chosen the immediate reward were asked to give reasons, 68% changed their choice to wait for two candy bars tomorrow. When they were just told another student selected differently but were not asked to give reasons, only 18% changed.6

Later Academic Outcomes

Mischel and his colleagues found seconds of delay time in preschool were significantly related to scores on the Scholastic Aptitude Test (SAT) later in high school. Children who waited longer (i.e., exhibited more patience) as preschoolers did significantly better on the most commonly used college entrance examination.7

The researchers also found the preschoolers who were told to think "fun" thoughts were able to wait longer but did not necessarily obtain higher SAT scores.

The children who could delay longer without being told to distract themselves did have significantly higher SAT scores.

Central Points

1. The ability to delay gratification, as measured by Walter Mischel's classic marshmallow experiments, appears to be related to several important outcomes later in life.

2. Kids who could wait longer were described by their parents ten years later as being more academically and socially competent, able to resist temptation and cope with stress, and more verbally fluent and attentive.

3. Kids who were given encouragement to distract themselves from thoughts about consuming the treats were able to wait longer.

4. Children who waited longer did significantly better on the SAT.

3

You can learn many things
from children. How much
patience you have, for instance.
Franklin P. Jones

The Attention-Deficit Hyperactivity Disorder Explosion

The fastest growing childhood disorder is a complex set of symptoms known as attention-deficit hyperactivity disorder (ADHD). In fact, the diagnosis of this condition has exploded to the extent that one might think it's an epidemic. However, we believe that the increase in ADHD also has a cultural factor.

Children are being raised with very little patience and limited ability to delay gratification. Then, in a school setting, children are asked to sit still and pay attention.

20

This may be the first time in their lives they haven't had some type of stimulation to occupy their minds. Expecting the excitement of video games or television, all they get is a teacher. Sometimes children develop the skill of patience on their own, sometimes their parents and teachers help them and sometimes they are quickly (and inappropriately) diagnosed as ADHD.

According to the criteria in the DSM-IV (Diagnostic and Statistical Manual of Mental Disorders, Fourth Edition of the American Psychiatric Association), to diagnose a child as having ADHD, he or she must display at least eight of the following characteristics for six months or more.

1. Fidgets, squirms or seems restless
2. Has difficulty remaining seated
3. Is easily distracted
4. Has difficulty awaiting turn
5. Blurts out something
6. Has difficulty following instructions
7. Has difficulty sustaining attention
8. Shifts from one uncompleted task to another
9. Has difficulty playing quietly
10. Talks excessively
11. Interrupts or intrudes on others
12. Does not seem to listen
13. Often loses things necessary for tasks
14. Frequently engages in dangerous actions

To be a case of ADHD, the onset of these behaviors must occur before the age of seven.

There is another "type" of attention disorder known as Undifferentiated Attention Deficit Disorder which is also referred to as attention-deficit disorder or ADD without hyperactivity. In this form, the most significant characteristic is inattentiveness. Hyperactivity is *not* present. These children also manifest problems with organization and distractibility but they are often quiet and reserved. It is this form of ADD that is most often missed because the classic behaviors associated with hyperactivity are not present. However, these children are at even greater risk of academic failure since they are often labeled "lazy," "daydreamers," or "unmotivated" when, in fact, they have an undiagnosed and, therefore, untreated condition.

If you believe your child may be suffering from ADHD/ADD, please seek an assessment. A good place to start would be at school. It's an excellent idea to consult with your child's teachers and other professionals such as the school psychologist, counselor and/or school nurse.

A Cautionary Note

Keep in mind, ADHD also happens to be the most mislabeled and overly diagnosed childhood problem in America today. We have worked with numerous children misdiagnosed as having ADHD. At the start of this chapter ADHD was described as *a complex set of symptoms*, but that does not mean every child with this collection of behaviors has ADHD. Other circumstances or disorders can produce very similar behaviors in children.

During certain stages of development, a majority of children will display some of the symptoms of ADHD such as inattention, hyperactivity, or impulsivity. For example, most adolescents go through a period where they are disorganized and rebellious. If the behaviors exhibited during this period of adolescence were not observed before the age of seven, it is not a case of ADHD.

Stress in children and adolescents can produce symptoms such as irritability, restlessness, and difficulty concentrating. Family difficulties such as divorce, remarriage, physical/emotional abuse, or the death of a family member will produce massive stress that can resemble ADHD.

Children who are anxious or depressed can exhibit very similar behaviors. Anxious and depressed children will fidget, squirm, seem restless, appear easily distracted, and have difficulties following instructions. It may also be difficult for them to sustain attention.

Similarly, young children will exhibit many of the behaviors associated with ADHD. Our daughter, age four, will shift from one uncompleted task to another, interrupts others, and at times does not seem to listen. This doesn't mean Anna has ADHD because almost all four-year-old children behave in a similar manner from time to time. What's important is the *degree* to which the behavior is *excessive* or *inappropriate* for the child's age.

A Final Cautionary Note

If you are planning on having an evaluation of your son or daughter to determine if ADHD might be present, we would recommend that you steer clear of the so-called "ADHD Clinics." A multidisciplinary, or "M-team" approach is a better way to examine the problem. The M-team goes into every evaluation giving equal weight to other potential disorders **and** to the possibility that the child is absolutely normal.

On initial consideration it may seem wise to go to a

clinic that specializes in ADHD since the people working there are obviously experienced with the disorder. However, when you go to an "ADHD Clinic" what disorder is the specialist going to find? When you go to a podiatrist, where are the problems likely to be found?

Please don't think we are questioning the character of the professionals who work at clinics which specialize in the diagnosis and treatment of ADHD. However, in our combined careers working in schools, we have observed an overwhelming majority (over 95%) of the children referred for evaluation to ADHD clinics come back diagnosed as ADHD. Wouldn't it seem somewhat strange if 95% of the children who had an eye examination needed glasses?

Let us once again say we are not accusing anyone of deliberately misdiagnosing children. Our explanation for this phenomenon has to do with preconceived expectations of findings.

The ADHD Surge

In 1970 there were 150,000 cases of ADHD in the United States. That figured soared to five million in 1997.1 The speed at which ADHD is being diagnosed recently caused problems for the manufacturer of Ritalin, the most commonly prescribed medication used to treat ADHD.

Ritalin is a controlled substance and as such, the amount manufactured needs to be approved by the federal government. In the mid 1990s there was a crisis in America as parts of the country literally ran out of Ritalin.

Ciba-Geigy, the manufacturer, had made a prediction regarding the amount of Ritalin necessary to satisfy demand based on the number of children taking the medication and the predicted rate of new cases. However, there were so many new diagnoses during that year the company ran out of the drug. Ciba-Geigy had to seek permission to produce more of the medication to meet the demand. Between the years 1970 and 1997 Ritalin production has increased 700 percent.

The Cause

This brings about an interesting question. Is there really an epidemic of ADHD or is something else responsible for this trend?

ADHD is a complex set of symptoms believed to be the result of a neurochemical imbalance or an underarousal of certain areas of the brain. Physically, kid's brains are basically the same now as they were in the 1960s. It's implausible to think the huge increase in ADHD is the result of sudden changes in the brains of children across this country.

Some would argue that the increase is due to improvements in diagnostic techniques. It is certainly true that physicians and psychologists have become increasingly adept at identifying ADHD, but that still does not account for the huge explosion of ADHD diagnoses. There must be something else to account for this trend.

The Legitimacy of ADHD

We would never support those who contend that ADHD is not a "real" disorder, though there are growing number of professionals who dismiss ADHD as a myth. Having worked with hundreds of kids who suffer from ADHD, we believe it is a disorder in the same manner as a learning disability. There are children with classic ADHD who find it nearly impossible to sit still, pay attention, and wait their turn. For many of these kids, Ritalin has worked wonders and given them control over their lives.

But why have the number of ADHD cases continued to grow and grow? It is appears as if ADHD were a contagious disease (which it is not). As stated previously, the brains of children are not changing on massive proportions.

The increase in ADHD is a cultural phenomenon. **We are raising children with little patience and limited ability to delay gratification.** Kids who never have to wait for anything are suddenly in an academic setting where patience is required. Children in school are asked to sit still and pay attention, often for the first time in their lives. There are no flashing lights or pulsating music from television or video games. There is just a teacher. Of all the things they have learned in their lives, they have never learned how to tolerate something that isn't all that exciting. They've never learned how to be patient. And that is where this book comes in.

Central Points

1. The fastest growing childhood disorder is a complex set of symptoms known as attention-deficit hyperactivity disorder (ADHD). The onset of these behaviors occurs before the age of seven.

2. During certain stages of development, a majority of children will display some of the symptoms of ADHD

such as inattention, hyperactivity, or impulsivity.

3. Children who are anxious or depressed can exhibit very similar behaviors. Similarly, young children will exhibit many of the behaviors associated with ADHD.

4. The increase in ADHD is largely a cultural phenomenon.

4

Perhaps the most valuable
result of all education is
the ability to make yourself
do the thing you have to do,
when it ought to be done,
whether you like it or not.
Thomas Henry Huxley

Patience and Low Frustration Tolerance

Jeff is 10 years old and attends fourth grade. He loves soccer, video games, and candy. Jeff is naturally bright; however, his teachers are concerned because he doesn't stop and think about the answers he writes out on tests and homework.

It seems everything is about speed. There is even some competition between Jeff and his classmates. During work periods, they glance around the room, trying to be the first student to complete the work. In fact, Jeff usually raises his arm in a sign of victory as he scribbles the last answer on his paper.

However, in Jeff's effort to complete the assignment first, he doesn't stop to think about his work. For Jeff, it's speed rather than quality that matters most. And the relief of having the assignment completed frees Jeff to think about other things, write notes, or bother his classmates.

This pattern of behavior continues at home in almost everything Jeff does. While cleaning his room for weekly chores, Jeff throws toys and shoes in the closet, puts dirty clothes under the bed, then rushes off to finish his Nintendo game.

Jeff's parents require homework to be completed before the TV can be turned on. What they don't realize is that Jeff often writes the easiest answer on his paper or simply copies from an encyclopedia to complete his homework quickly.

Jeff also gets angry when things don't move along as quickly as he would expect. If he has to work with his sister to do the dishes, he often complains as she carefully rinses each dish before placing it in the dishwasher.

For Jeff, and millions of other kids, it's all about having the frustration stop. "No more work. Now I'm free to think about me and what I want to do," is what children like Jeff believe.

This characteristic in children who lack patience is known as low frustration tolerance (LFT). LFT can be defined as an unwillingness, *not an inability*, to tolerate frustrating events. It's really all about patience and teaching children, even in this accelerated society, that quality and satisfying results come when we take the time to do the job carefully the first time.

Every child *can* tolerate frustration. In fact, there are many instances in their lives when they simply have no choice but to deal with disappointment. For example, all kids occasionally get hungry 30 minutes before meal time and have to deal with the frustration of the hunger for a short time. We've all been at the grocery store with our kids in the slowest moving line when there simply isn't a choice but to wait.

On the other hand, there are some frustrating situations in which there is the possibility for avoidance or escape. Doing homework is a good example. Kids like Jeff and millions more always have the choice of closing the book. There may be consequences later but they still have the choice at that moment to continue or stop.

LFT and School

LFT is a common problem in education because schooling involves many frustrating events. It is virtually impossible to be successful in school without having the ability to tolerate at least a moderate amount of frustration. In the learning process, there is typically a point between partial comprehension and complete understanding that is very frustrating. It's the point where we don't quite "get it." Kids with LFT reach this point and simply give up in order to escape the frustration. They bail out at this crucial moment when, if they could persevere for just a few more seconds, things would clear up. This tendency quickly becomes a pattern that is hard to break.

The Persistence of LFT

The difficult thing about breaking the LFT tendency is that **it feels good to get out of a frustrating situation**. In effect, it is rewarding to give up. Jeff learns that over and over each day at school and at home. Kids like Jeff have learned to give into immediate gratification, but will pay the price later. Unfortunately, some students never learn to delay gratification.

The ability to tolerate frustration may not seem important but the ability to tolerate frustration and delay gratification are two of the most important factors in predicting outcomes later in life. Think of all the things that are worth having that can be obtained quickly and easily. It doesn't take long to finish that list does it? Now reverse the equation and think of the things that take time and are frustrating to acquire. Professional degrees, successful businesses, nice homes, and most significant successes take time, effort, and dedication. Along the way there are inevitable set backs and numerous disappointments, but to reach an important goal or obtain success you have to refocus yourself and keep working. Kids (and adults) who suffer from LFT have not learned this lesson.

Talking Sense to Yourself

The pattern of avoiding frustration affects virtually every aspect of children's lives. This type of thinking becomes ingrained in children and works into their internal dialogue or self-talk—that "little voice" we hear in the back of our head or in our "mind's ear." People talk to themselves whether they are aware of it or not. This self-talk contains the personal philosophies about the world that guide our behaviors and influences the decisions we make.

When working with students who have difficulties with LFT, we use a specific method of counseling known as Rational-Emotive Behavior Therapy (REBT). REBT helps kids to focus on their self-talk and determine whether or not this internal dialogue makes sense. Does the message lead to good or bad results? Is there evidence to support the beliefs and ideas contained in this self-talk? If so, the beliefs are probably helpful. If the beliefs are not supported by evidence, the ideas are probably doing harm. (There will be more information about self-talk in a later chapter on anger management.)

Common Beliefs in LFT

Students who suffer from LFT all seem to hold one common, highly irrational belief. They erroneously believe, **"Life should always be easy and without frustration."** Obviously, life is not easy and contains a great deal of frustration. Life is actually spelled H-A-S-S-L-E. Don't get us wrong, it would be nice if life were free of frustration, but it isn't and probably never will be. Wishing or demanding that life be any different certainly does nothing to change reality.

LFT can manifest itself in many forms in school-aged children. Educational psychologist William Knaus[1] proposed that when the following behaviors are observed, LFT may be a primary or contributing factor:

    1) Whining
    2) Complaining

3) Day-dreaming

4) Lack of responsibility

5) Withdrawal or shyness

Knaus went on to make the point that many commonly occurring childhood problems such as eating disorders, poor impulse control, compulsive disorders, anxiety disorders, and conduct disorders all have one thing in common: low frustration tolerance. If children exhibit tendencies associated with one or more of the above mentioned problems, suspect that LFT is a contributing factor to the child's difficulties.

More LFT Beliefs

As mentioned earlier, the idea that "Life should always be easy and without frustration" is a belief that is typically at the core of LFT. However, there are other irrational ideas that many impatient children hold that also interfere with their academic progress. Bard and Fischer[2] examined a number of these irrational beliefs that lead to problems:

1) **"Things will turn out OK whether I work or not,"** rather than the rational belief, "How things turn out depends to a large extent on what I do. I can choose to avoid working, but I realize that by not working I am probably creating a situation that I will be forced to deal with at a later date."

2) **"Everything should be entertaining and enjoyable and no unpleasantness should occur whatsoever,"** rather than the rational belief, "It would be nice if everything was entertaining but that is unrealistic.

33

Life just isn't like that."

     3) **"This is too hard...too much...too boring and I can't stand it,"** rather than the rational belief, "Some things are difficult and boring but people can certainly stand boredom. No one has ever died from boredom."

Overcoming LFT

     How can you improve children's abilities to tolerate frustration? Start by pointing out the consequences of their decisions and actions. When kids are grounded for poor academic work or missed assignments, trace the problem back to when they originally made a poor decision. Explain in a calm, matter-of-fact fashion that it wasn't Mrs. Smith's fault when the child chose not to study for the mid-term examination. The student chose to go to the movies instead of studying.

     Another intervention that might be effective is to simply ask the student if he or she believes some of the earlier mentioned beliefs such as, "Life should always be easy and without frustration." If the student says "No," explain that you asked because his or her behavior suggested it. Putting off assignments and not studying seems to indicate that a student *does* believe, "Life should always be easy and without frustration." Finally, ask them what the long term results would be if a person lived by the belief, "Life should always be easy and without frustration." At the very least you'll spend some additional time talking with your son or daughter and that's something we all could do more of anyway.

     If kids do believe, "Life should always be fair and

34

without frustration," ask them for proof that this idea is true. Help them to make a connection between this belief and the problems they are having in life.

The Power of Positive Self-Talk

There is one final technique for helping your child overcome difficulties with LFT. See if you can recognize when a child is talking to himself (i.e., when his "tapes" are playing) about "how boring or stupid school work is and how it shouldn't be so hard." Try to get him to interrupt this dialogue and substitute a new thought. For example, just repeating a simple phrase such as, "I can do it" can be extremely beneficial. It gives the student self-confidence but, more importantly, it blocks out all the negative self-talk. Following is an example of how you might help a child "switch tapes."

Adult: "What are you working on there, Jeff?"

Student: "Science."

A: "How is it going?"

S: "Not very good. I don't really like science. It's boring."

A: "You know what? Every class has some parts to it that are more fun than other parts. Not every assignment can be fun and interesting."

S: "I suppose you're right but I still think this assignment is especially stupid."

A: "Is that what you are thinking to yourself right now while you are trying to work?"

S: "Yeah. This assignment is stupid and I don't know why I have to do it."

A: "Can you agree with what I just said a minute ago that all classes will have assignments that may not be as interesting as other assignments?"

S: "Yes."

A: "Then this is probably one of those assignments and what you need to do now is work through it the best way you can. Do you think that telling yourself, 'This assignment is stupid and I don't know why I have to do it' will help you do a good job or make it harder to do a good job?"

S: "I think it just makes me hate doing it that much more."

A: "You're exactly right. What would happen if you told yourself something like this, 'I can do it even if I think it's boring' or 'I can deal with this even though I don't like it?'"

S: "I'd probably be able to have a better attitude."

A: "Do me a favor and when you hear yourself thinking 'how stupid this is,' try stopping yourself and thinking something else like, 'I can deal with this even though I don't like it.' It will be sort of our experiment."

The Egg Timer Technique

I (PW) spent several years as a math teacher with students ranging from middle school to college age. During this time, I noticed that students who struggle in math (like Jeff) have a tendency to rush through assignments. It was as if their first priority was simply having all the problems completed. If the answers happened to be correct, that was an unexpected bonus.

While teaching middle school students, I developed a policy with class assignments that considerably improved the performance of most students. I would estimate the

36

amount of time an assignment would take, for example, 15 minutes. I would then explain to the class that if *everyone* was working for the full 15 minutes, they would earn some free time for Friday. Even if they rushed through their work and were done in five minutes, I expected them to recheck their work for the rest of the time remaining if they were to earn the free time.

After a few days the kids who rushed through their assignments realized they might as well slow down and do it right the first time since they would be working for 15 minutes anyway. The students also kept each other working because they all had to follow the rules to get the reward.

The results were impressive. Not only did their daily homework grades improve considerably (I expected that), they did much better on examinations because they were learning more.

Parents can duplicate this same process with kids at home. Simply make a judgment regarding the amount of time it will take to do a good job on an assignment. If you don't feel comfortable making that judgment, ask the teacher to write it down on the top of the assignment.

Next have the child work in an area that you can monitor because they need to be *working*, not daydreaming. Then agree upon an appropriate reward if the child works for the entire time. Finally, get out the egg timer and you're ready to go.

We expect you'll get results similar to those I had in class. Not only will your child earn some type of small reward but he or she will also observe the pay off in terms of better grades. And that's the whole idea. When the student starts getting rewarded with better grades, you hope his/her new, patient behavior can continue by itself without the need for monitoring.

Central Points

1. Low Frustration Tolerance can be defined as "an unwillingness to tolerate frustrating events."

2. LFT is a common problem in education because schooling involves many frustrating events.

3. LFT can easily become a pattern because kids are immediately rewarded by giving up.

4. Kids who suffer from LFT often hold beliefs such as, "Life should always be easy and without frustration" and "Things will turn out OK whether I work or not."

5. To overcome LFT, parents are encouraged to help kids make connections between the poor choices they make and the consequences of those choices.

6. Using simple, self-affirming statements such as, "I can do this" can be very helpful in blocking out the negative thinking.

7. The frustration felt by many impatient children often leads to other problems, such as academic underachievement, which will be examined next.

5

The greatest power is
often simple patience.
　　E. Joseph Conrad

The Consequences of Impatience

So what do we know about the impatient child?
Like Jeff (described in Chapter 4), the impatient child looks
for the immediate reward rather than the consequences
down the road.

But what are the results of this lack of patience? Are
the consequences short-lived or do they follow the child
into adulthood?

Usually, the problem is first recognized in school. A
solid academic career requires the ability to tolerate
frustration and boredom. Let's face it, there isn't a teacher
alive who can make punctuation exercises as exciting as a
video game. To be successful in school, kids need to learn
to persevere when things get tough, boring, frustrating, and
tiresome. Impatient children often struggle to do this.

Impatience Does Not Discriminate

The only pattern regarding impatient children is that there is no consistent prototype. Impatience doesn't discriminate. It affects both boys and girls, black and white, rich and poor. Impatience is found in the gifted kids and the intellectually challenged. Many impatient children can also be described as suffering from what is known as underachievement syndrome.

What is Underachievement?

It seems like a simple question—what is underachievement? Taken at face value, the question is very easy to answer. Underachievement is achieving at a level below one's potential. However, it gets a little more complicated when we take a step back and consider some broader issues.

For example, are all children who score below their current grade placement underachievers? If we looked at a typical class of 24 second-grade students and found seven scoring below second-grade level in reading, could we say that they are underachievers? The answer is "no."

In another example, if we examined a class of 29 high school freshmen (ninth graders) who were all scoring at a junior level (eleventh grade), could we conclude that none of these students are underachievers? The answer again is "no."

The reason we cannot assume that the below-grade-level second graders and the above-grade-level ninth graders are not underachievers is that we do not know their *potential*. If in the first scenario, the below-grade-level second graders had significantly impaired intellects (i.e., were mentally handicapped), they could not be considered underachievers. Even if they were a full year behind their current grade placement (i.e., reading at a first grade level), they still might be performing at an expected level given their ability.

Conversely, if the freshmen who are performing at a junior level were extremely bright, we might predict them to be even further ahead. By definition, even though these students are performing two years ahead of their current grade placement, they could still be achieving below their ability. So **underachievement can be thought of as a discrepancy between students' academic potential and their actual achievement.** More specifically, underachievement is achievement below a student's academic potential.

The Long-Term Consequences of Underachievement

One of the most extensive and ambitious studies of underachievers ever attempted was conducted in 1981 by Otto, Call, and Spenner.[1] The authors contacted over 6,599 subjects 13 years after high school. All had been identified as underachievers as juniors and seniors in the years 1965-66. The authors found that underachievers were less likely to have finished college and completed fewer years of post-secondary education than achievers of the same mental ability. Underachievers were almost twice as likely to have attended vocational or technical school, but only half as likely to have attend a college or university.

Employment

Thirteen years after high school, underachievers held jobs of lower status than achieving students of the same mental ability. Underachievers held jobs of equal status with students who earned similar grades but were not considered underachievers as their grades matched their abilities.

Wages

Underachievers earned less money after high school than did achieving students of the same ability. Underachieving males earned $.76 less per hour than achieving students of the same ability, which translates into 7.7% less pay. Underachieving females earned $.73 less per hour or 12.2% less pay.

Career Changes

Underachievers held more jobs in the thirteen years following high school when compared with students with similar mental abilities. This fact lends support for the premise that underachievers have a difficult time tolerating frustration. When a job becomes frustrating or boring, the underachiever "bails out" just as they learned to do while enrolled in school.

Do Underachievers Catch Up?

Some underachievers did eventually catch up educationally and occupationally to students who had similar academic potential. It was noted, however, that underachievers who were two or more grade levels below expectancies did not catch up with students of similar ability. These students only attained educational and occupational levels consistent with students with similar grade point averages. McCloskey, Evahn, and Kratzer[2] noted that if students were below expectations by only a grade or two, came from highly educated parents, and possessed self-confidence, they were much more likely to catch up to peers with similar abilities. Without these characteristics, it appears underachievement is a relatively permanent condition.

If your child is experiencing academic difficulties, help is on the way. There will be an entire chapter devoted to activities to enhance school performance later in this book.

Social Difficulties

Impatient children often have difficulty interacting with other children. Social interaction is, by its very nature, a give and take process. For relationships to survive, both parties must benefit.

What happens to children who always want things to be "their" way? Eventually, other kids get tired of playing with them. Their companions feel cheated and don't want to play over at Sara's house because "she doesn't play nice."

Think for a moment. What do kids mean when they say "she doesn't play nice?" Usually it has to do with another child's unwillingness to:

1) take turns
2) share
3) let others tell their ideas
4) let others choose an activity

All of the above-mentioned items require patience. When kids don't have patience, they usually don't have a lot of friends either.

Long-Term Social Consequences

Perhaps the most striking finding in the study by Otto, Call, and Spenner was that underachievers were 50% *more likely to divorce* in the thirteen years following high school. This percentage was higher than either comparison group (i.e., students who had similar mental abilities and students who had similar grades).

This tendency to have failed marriages is likely to be the result of poor relationship skills learned as children. It is also related to the impatient adult's inability to tolerate the frustration that all marriages go through from time to time. There are no perfect marriages except on the silver screen. When the relationship experiences some normal rough spots, adults with little or no ability to tolerate frustration look for a way out.

Central Points

Impatient children tend to have more difficulties in school than their peers. The list of difficulties extends well past the school years to employment and relationship issues. Recall that underachievers tend to:

1) hold jobs of lower status than achieving students of the same mental ability
2) earn less money after high school than achieving students of the same ability
3) change jobs more frequently
4) experience more relationship problems as

children
5) have a 50% greater chance of being divorced

6

The secret of success is constancy of purpose.
Benjamin Disraeli

Teaching Children to Talk to Themselves

We all know people who are patient. These folks are usually the quiet type who don't holler when they're hungry, or complain when they have to wait in line. They usually let others take the comfortable chair and are always willing to help with the dirty work.

However, we often talk about this characteristic as if it were encoded into their DNA. Like blue eyes and blonde hair, hairy knuckles or a cleft chin, we tend to think these qualities just happen, that these people were just born patient.

So naturally, the question arises, "Can you teach kids to be patient?" It's a fair question. We believe, and evidence from controlled studies suggests, the answer is yes. Now let's systematically explain how to do it.

46

Thought and Behavior

Before we can start to alter a child's conduct we must first understand what drives behavior in the first place. Why do kids do the things they do? What guides and directs a child's behavior?

The great Russian neuropsychologist L.S. Vygotsky suggested that the internalization of verbal commands is *the* critical step in the child's development of voluntary control of his or her behavior.1 In other words, kids direct their behavior using their "self-talk." Kids, like adults, talk to themselves internally and it is this inner dialogue that directs their behavior.

This self-talk is produced in a part of the brain known as the frontal lobes. Other prominent scientists have demonstrated that when brain damage occurs in the areas that control internal verbalizations (i.e., self-talk), patients have difficulties with impulsivity and goal-directed behavior in general.2 In other words, when brain mechanisms controlling self-talk are damaged, behavior tends to be more impulsive and less thoughtful.

Keep in mind that we often do not hear this little voice. It's nearly automatic—sort of like breathing. We talk to ourselves (and breath) all day long, but usually aren't aware of it. That doesn't mean these mechanisms aren't functioning. Try to get through just a single day without talking to yourself (or breathing). It's not possible.

Since we know what guides children's behavior, it makes sense to teach them how to use self-talk in a positive way. A proven program to help kids with impulsive behavior is called **Self-Instructional Training (SIT)**. As the title suggests, it is a program designed to teach kids to modify their behavior by talking to themselves.

Self-Instructional Training (SIT)

SIT is a four step process that requires the help and guidance of an adult. The first step is to select a task to use during the teaching portion of this program. You might want to use a dot-to-dot or maze game. Success in these tasks requires a lot of patience.

Step One - The adult does a maze while talking aloud to himself or herself about the strategy to use. For example, the adult may be saying something such as:

> "I have to go slowly to get it right.
> Look down this row and see if it's
> the right one. No, I'll be trapped
> by the wall if I go there. How about
> this one? Yes, that one leads all
> the way out. Good, I'm going very
> slow and being careful. I'm doing a good
> job."

It's also a good idea to intentionally make a mistake and model how to cope with that.

> "I'm going to go down this one.
> Oops. That's not the right one.
> I made a mistake because I didn't
> go slow and check all the way until
> the end. That's okay. I'll be
> sure to find the right one this

time."

Step 2 - Let the child use the pencil now to do a similar maze. The adult is to talk aloud guiding the child's work. The same type of verbalizations are to be used. Praise the child for following your lead and doing the maze correctly.

Step 3 - Now let the child practice on a similar maze, but instead of you talking the child through it, tell the child to talk (aloud) to himself or herself while working on the maze. The adult should remind the child to "go slowly" and "check all the way before you go down an alley." Praise the child for using self-talk and for exhibiting patience on the maze.

Let kids practice several mazes this way until they get used to talking aloud while they work. Do as many mazes as you feel is necessary before proceeding.

Step 4 - Now it's time for the child to do the maze while talking silently to himself or herself. Just as before, remind the child to "go slowly" and "be careful." This time their verbalizations are only in their head.

This type of program has been proven to be effective with impulsive children. Children given this type of direct instruction have demonstrated better performance on the non-verbal portion of intelligence tests, and have decreased impulsivity and shown fewer errors on other measures of performance.[3] What's most encouraging is that this improved performance was maintained after the direct instruction was discontinued.

So, to answer the question once again, "Can you teach kids to be less impulsive and more patient?" The answer is, "Yes, you can."

We really like SIT but there are other programs that teach these skills. "Stop and Think" by Phillip Kendall also helps children cope with impatience and impulsivity.

More Examples

Now, let's try a real-life problem. For example, in baseball only one person can be the batter at a time. The others must play the field. Let's see how to use SIT to work through this problem.

Step 1 - An adult decides to play baseball with the kids. He or she could mention how much fun it will be to be the batter. Then the stage would be set for self-talk like this:

> "The rules are that only one person
> gets to be the batter. If we all take
> turns everyone will get a chance to bat.
> If I get mad and decide 'If I can't be
> first, I'm not playing,' I won't get
> my turn."

Step 2 - The child who is playing in the field would have to have the modeling adult close by. The adult could direct self-calming statements like the ones above at the child.

Step 3 - The adult would stand behind the child who is pitching and encourage him or her to use patience-inducing self-talk. The adult could praise the child for attempting to use self-talk.

Step 4 - At this point the child is to be using the self-talk internally. The adult's only task is to remind the child to do so.

It is wise to practice SIT extensively with exercises like mazes or dot-to-dot before trying to implement such a program in real life. Kids and adults have a very human tendency to fall back on old habits if there hasn't been a lot of practice prior to actually using this program. The practice of SIT will pay off when it becomes time to transfer this program into true experiences.

Additional Applications and Examples

Assume a child is working on homework or making model cars. Remaining patient through the process is essential if the child is interested in a good outcome.

Step 1 - The adult would sit down at the table to make certain things are going as planned. The stage would be set for self-talk like this:

> "To do a good job I need to take
> my time. The slower I go the
> better I do. If I want this to
> be right, I have to slow down."

Step 2 - The adult is to talk aloud guiding the child's work. The same type of verbalizations as above are to be used. The adult praises the child for using SIT and doing the task correctly.

Step 3 - Stay near the child as he or she uses the self-talk to guide his or her behavior. Make certain the child is doing the self-talk correctly.

Step 4 - At this point the child is to be using the self-talk internally. The adult's only task is to remind the child to do so.

Use of a Signal Word

One of the shortcomings of the SIT program has to do with its reliance on adults to model proper behavior. It isn't practical to expect adults to be able to constantly model patient behavior and remind kids to use self-talk. Too many situations would not allow it.

However, what you can do is teach children a signal word that an adult or the children can use as a reminder. For example, when you see the child in a situation where impulsive behavior is likely to occur, use a signal word as a reminder for the child to use SIT. The signal word should be something not commonly found in everyday language like "jabberwocky" or "moose mustache".

You might observe the child doing homework at the kitchen table and note some mounting frustration. Rather than going into a long discussion of the importance of using their self-talk, you simply say "moose mustache" as the reminder word and this cues the child to use the SIT plan. It would also be wise to stay fairly close by to intervene if the child continues to struggle with the homework. Also, teach your kids to signal themselves as a reminder to use SIT whenever they have some type of difficult task ahead, whether it be academic or otherwise. If they are of school age, every time they receive an assignment in school they should be using SIT. The point of all this is to have SIT become second nature. It will take practice, reminders, and more practice, but SIT is a skill children can use the rest of their lives.

Central Points

1. SIT is a step-by-step program that teaches children to slow down their normally impatient style of responding by talking to themselves.

2. It is best if the SIT model is taught using situations such as mazes before attempts are made to expand the practice to real-life situations.

3. It is essential to remember that helping children learn to apply such a skill is a major undertaking.

4. SIT will not be successful if it is not consistently encouraged and reinforced.

7

A child miseducated
is a child lost.
John F. Kennedy

Solving the Impatient
Child's School Problems

A good education is one of the most precious gifts we
can give children. In fact, at the time of this writing, we
are deciding whether or not Anna (she has the dreaded late
summer birthday) should attend kindergarten this fall, or
wait another year. There are several options, and we are
carefully weighing the pros and cons. We realize that a good
start can mean the difference between success and failure in
school. Most parents feel this way, too.

We all realize that poor school adjustment can lead
to academic problems, which can hinder future career
opportunities. Difficulties in school can also harm a child's
self-confidence and hamper the development of social
relationships. Simply put, an exemplary educational

experience lays the ground work for success later in life.

The Early Years

However, as aware as parents may be, problems often do not become apparent until they are very BIG problems. In fact, many impatient children do not experience academic problems during the first few years of school. Many impatient kids also happen to be bright, which allows them to rush through assignments and still do a majority of the work correctly. If there are concerns at school during the early elementary years, they tend to be more behavioral in nature.

As children enter fourth and fifth grade, their impatience starts to cause more difficulties due to these facts:

1) Assignments become longer. Kids have to persevere through some difficulties to finish the work. Students with low frustration tolerance can find a million things to do *other* than complete school work.

2) It is around fourth and fifth grade that students are expected to work independently. Since the teacher isn't working directly with the students, it is much easier for them to daydream and quietly avoid work.

Academic Signs of Impatience

What types of school behaviors suggest impatience? Here are the few tendencies that suggest impatience may be a problem:

1) **Rushes through work.** The most tell-tale sign students with difficulties related to low frustration tolerance

is the tendency to work too quickly. Their performance is marked by numerous mistakes on problems they know how to do correctly.

2) **Starts but doesn't finish assignments.** This is especially noticeable as the assignments get longer.

3) **Difficulties with organization.** It takes time and effort to stay organized. The locker typically is a mess of half-finished assignments as well as papers that should have been taken home long ago.

4) **Difficulties with directions.** Impatient children often start doing assignments before they have completely heard or read the directions. They are in such a hurry to get an assignment completed that they don't follow the directions correctly.

Steps to Take If Trouble Starts

What can you do to help an impatient child if school starts to become a problem? **The first, and by far the most important, step is for parents and educators to work together.** Rarely can any significant school problem be corrected without cooperation between home and school.

Home and School Cooperation

It is a good idea to let the child's teacher(s) know you are concerned. This allows the teacher and other school employees (school counselor, psychologist, social worker) to keep a closer eye on the child. Chances are they are already aware of the problem, but when parents are obviously concerned, educators are a little more focused on the child. Not that teachers aren't concerned about all kids, but the squeaky wheel gets the grease in schools, too.

If you're concerned about the child's inability to finish work or the poor quality of the work, contact his or her teacher and start a dialogue. Most of the time, the school will be glad to hear from you.

If you have already been discussing the problem with your child's teacher and things are still not going well, it's time to get together for a face-to-face meeting. Sometimes waiting until regularly scheduled parent-teacher conferences is just too long.

Parent/Teacher Meetings

Once a parent/teacher meeting has been scheduled, it's important for the parents to be clear regarding their objectives. If there is no set agenda of what is to be accomplished, it is possible for such meetings to degenerate into "the blame game" in which the parents blame the school for not doing a better job with their child and the school employees blame the parents for not supporting their efforts. This adult version of "hot potato" is a common problem and, unfortunately, keeps the focus away from the intent of the meeting which should be 1) to gather and share information, and 2) to start formulating a multi-dimensional, multi-faceted plan to get the child back on track.

Write It Down!

It is a good idea to have someone at this meeting be a recorder or note taker. Many times excellent plans are formulated at these meetings but there is no clear understanding of who is responsible for each planned intervention. If someone is taking notes, the results of the meeting can be summarized before all parties leave. Copies can be made and handed out.

Parents may feel uncomfortable at a school meeting. Teachers may describe problems with their children which can be hard to hear. Hopefully, teachers will be kind and tactful. Be warned, however, that if parents feel frustrated with their child's performance, his or her teachers are probably also frustrated.

Questions to Ask

It may be helpful to prepare a list of questions to remind yourself of the points you want to cover. Here are some suggestions:

1) What seems to be the cause of my child's grade in math? reading? etc.
2) What can I do as a parent to help?
3) When does he/she ask for help in class?
4) When does he/she appear to be paying attention in class? How can this be explained?
5) When does he/she seem to be rushing through his/her work? How can this be explained?
6) When does he/she participate in class discussion?
7) When is his/her work turned in on time?
8) When does my child follow directions?
9) Is the problem with test scores, daily assignments, or both?
10) Is there a need for a follow-up meeting to determine how well the current plan is working?

Reports Home

In order to coordinate communication between home and school, it is recommended that some type of routine report be sent home to the parents from the child's teachers. When school and parents keep in close contact, many of the avenues that students use to avoid work are simply no longer available. The proverbial oldest trick in the book (i.e., "I did all my work at school") will no longer be a possibility. Other advantages of reports coming home are:

1) Reports require parents and teachers to work together so neither party is solely responsible for solving the problems.
2) Notes home provide parents with frequent information on the student's progress.
3) Students often appreciate and respond to the added information regarding their performance.
4) Notes can include positive information about effort and achievement which can encourage the student to remain committed to improvement.

Notes home are also an excellent means of keeping in close contact regarding non-academic concerns. If the child is upset about something that occurred at home, teachers can be made aware of that fact and, hopefully, can be a little more sensitive during the day. Schools really appreciate any type of forewarning that can be given or information that might help avoid problems.

Behavioral Contracts

It is a good idea to set up a simple behavioral

contract to allow these children to receive little rewards when they have a "good" day at school. With younger students, the teacher can use a report home that's as simple as a happy or sad face to convey the child's performance. With older children, a good or bad day can depend on the number of assignments they have completed and turned in to teachers. If they have completed all assignments appropriately, they can chose a small, daily reward such as a later bed time or reduced chores. They can also have the option of holding off on the daily rewards and saving their "good days" for a bigger reward at the end of the week. It's best to let these options be decided upon by the child, but the parents need to be able to live with the plan.

How often do these reports need to be sent home? Daily reports are best for elementary students. After a few weeks, if the system is working, it is always possible to decrease the frequency of the reports home. After a while, a Monday-Wednesday-Friday schedule can be used, and eventually just a weekly note home on Friday should suffice.

Don't forget that e-mail is an option in a lot of cases. E-mail is such a nice alternative to the actual paper and pencil note because there is no way a child can lose an e-mail message. And a dog has never, ever swallowed a piece of electronic mail either!

Eventually most children will no longer need a monitoring system using notes home or weekly phone calls. The goal is to develop the child's internal desire to do better simply because that will produce the best outcome. Eventually the values of hard work and self-respect will make the student want to succeed, not for the sake of the rewards, but for the feeling that comes only after a person has done his or her very best.

Following are a few other practical ideas you can use if impatience is starting to affect academic performance.

The Desert Principle

Never let children eat their ice cream before their carrots and the same suggestion holds true with school work. Don't let the child continue in the habit of "play then work." You can understand how this practice is not only detrimental in school, but in other facets of life as well. The culmination of good work habits is what we call "self-discipline." Try to find a successful person without it!

Some kids can come home right after school and do homework. If that's your child, consider yourself lucky! Most kids need time to decompress after school, just like most adults like to unwind when they get home from work. It may be best to give kids some time after school to play, relax and do whatever they choose before starting with school work. You may even prefer to wait until after dinner because you'll get better results.

A Homework Area

It's a good idea to have a designated area for homework. It should be a place that is quiet and free of distractions. If you're lucky, there is a place in the house that can be specifically designated as the homework area. In a lot of homes that is still the kitchen table, which is better than the child's bedroom because the kitchen is easier to supervise.

It's not a good idea to let kids listen to music when they study. Even though they say, "It helps me do better work," research suggests just the opposite. Music, especially the lyrics, distracts kids and interferes with concentration. Establish a rule that homework be done without music.

Homework Time

It may be wise to set up a predetermined time when homework is to be started. By setting a consistent time for homework, it's less likely to be left until the last minute.

The Egg Timer Technique Revisited

As was explained earlier, rushing through assignments is a common problem with impatient kids. Their first priority is simply to have all the problems completed. If the answers happened to be correct, that's an unexpected bonus!

Recall how the egg timer technique was used. First the teacher would estimate the amount of time an assignment would take, for example, 15 minutes. Next the teacher would explain to the class that if everyone was working for the full 15 minutes, students would earn free time on Friday. Even if some students rushed through their work and were done in five minutes, they were expected to recheck their work for the rest of the remaining time.

Students tend to keep each other working because they all have to follow the rules to get the rewards. After a few days, the kids who rushed through their assignments realized they might as well slow down and do it right the first time since they would be working for 15 minutes anyway.

Parents can duplicate this same program with kids at home. Start by making a judgment regarding the amount of time it will take to do an adequate job on an assignment. If you don't feel comfortable making that judgment, ask the teacher to write it down on the top of the assignment or in the assignment notebook.

Have the child work in an area that you can monitor because he or she needs to be *working*, not daydreaming. Next you need to agree upon some type of reward to be earned if he or she works for the entire time. Then get out the old egg timer and you're ready to go.

Hopefully, your child will earn some type of small reward and also see the payoff in terms of better grades— the goal in the first place. When a child's grades improve, an association will be made between his or her new, patient behavior and success.

Other Ideas to Encourage On Task Behavior

Check frequently to make certain the child is on task. Remember that just because children are sitting in front of books with pencils, it doesn't mean they are concentrating on work. Some impatient children can put on a convincing performance during homework time while not actually focusing on the task at hand. Stay close enough to check on their work.

Some kids will need more reminders to stay on task. These reminders can take different shapes. They don't necessarily have to sound like, "Why aren't you working?" Such questions sound punitive. It's better to ask, "How's your homework going?" which is an innocent question but still serves the purpose of refocusing the child.

Before turning children loose to work independently,

it's important to make certain they are capable of doing the work. They may be off task because they don't know how to work the problems. In such cases, off-task behavior isn't noncompliance, it's academic incompetence.

Get to know your child's learning strengths and weaknesses. Kids vary considerably in this regard. Some children take a while to get started but once they settle down to work they get a lot accomplished. Others can work for 15 minutes and need a short break. Schedule breaks often for these students.

Along this line, it's also a good idea to break up assignments into manageable chunks. Kids won't feel so overwhelmed. Students with low frustration tolerance can easily allow themselves to get swamped with work. They then find it easy to simply walk away with the attitude, "I can't do all this." If they had managed their schedules better, they would have been slowly working toward the final product from the beginning instead of procrastinating. That's where parents and teachers can help out.

It's also helpful to change learning modalities often. For example, if the student has a lot of reading to do, it would be wise to do some silent reading and some reading aloud. Reading to the child for a portion of the assignment would also be an appropriate change of pace.

Central Points

1. A good education is one of the most precious gifts we can give children. Success in school lays the ground work for achievement later in life.
2. One of the most important steps is for parents and educators to work together. This starts by

establishing ongoing communication between the home and school.

3. If your son or daughter is struggling in school, set up a meeting with his or her teacher(s).
4. Formulate a plan to get the child back on track.
5. Communicate on an ongoing basis either by phone, notes home, or e-mail.
6. It may be wise to have a designated homework time and work area.
7. Parents can help impatient children stay on task using a variety of practical techniques.

8

Never forget what
a man says to you
when he's angry.
Henry Ward Beecher

Coping with
Frustration and Anger

Think of the most impatient person you know. You would most likely say that person is frustrated and angry quite often, too. You know the type—the person who runs from check out to check out at the grocery store, searching for the fastest line; the person who darts from lane to lane in traffic; the person who paces or taps fingers on the table while waiting. This person, almost certainly, feels frustrated and angry many times during an average day. This person is frustrated and angry because the rest of the world does not move quickly enough.

Impatience, frustration, and anger—these emotions go hand in hand. One leads to the other. That's why this chapter on anger is important. If your child's impatience has

66

led to frustration, then to anger, it will be helpful for him or her to learn to stop before it spins out of control and becomes a common pattern.

In addition, the skills kids learn to manage their anger are an essential part of overall self-discipline.

What Causes Kids To Get Angry Anyway?

This is a very important question. Until we understand the "cause", how can we work toward a "cure"? What *really* causes kids to get ticked off?

Is it their parents?

Is it their brothers and sisters?

Is it their teachers?

Is it the full moon?

The answer to all these questions is NO.

No matter what people think, none of the things mentioned above can *make* kids angry. Children (and adults) control how they feel. So the answer to the million dollar question, "What makes kids angry?" is, "They do."

It may take time for children (and adults) to accept the idea that they are responsible for their feelings. The best way to start getting that point across is with analogies. Tell this story for starters.

"Let's pretend you were walking home from the library and somebody knocked all your books out of your hands. How would you feel? You'd probably be angry, right?

But when you turn around to see who hit your

books you realize it was a blind man who accidentally bumped into you. Now how would you feel? Still angry? Probably not."

It's essential that kids understand one important part of this story. The books were still knocked out of their hands so **things happening** (such as dropped books) don't make people angry. Anger must be caused by something else.

That "something else" is their *thoughts*. Their thoughts, beliefs, and ideas are what make them angry, not their parents, teachers or family.

Kids will need more convincing of this fact, so here is a more in-depth look at the book incident to emphasize the origin of their emotions.

What would you probably be thinking just as your books went flying?

_____

_____

_____

Could it be something like, "You clumsy jerk. Watch where you're going?" Those thoughts would definitely make anybody angry.

But what would you think to yourself when you saw it was a blind man?

_____

_____

_____

Maybe something like, "He didn't mean to do it. It was an accident." Those thoughts would calm you down.

Notice how the event (getting your books scattered) stayed the same but the feelings changed as your thoughts changed. That's because YOUR THOUGHTS INFLUENCE (and largely control) YOUR FEELINGS.

This is good news. If other people and things made us angry, what would be the point of trying to learn to handle our anger? There wouldn't be a point because YOU would have no control—other people would be controlling you like a puppet.

Also point out that if events made people angry, then everybody would be angry at the same things. The fact of the matter is people aren't angry at the same events. Things that tick off some people probably make others laugh, so it can't be "things" or other people that make people angry.

The next step is to help kids learn to start hearing their thoughts before they get angry. Not easy, but not impossible.

Strengthening the Connection Between Thoughts and Feelings

Below is an exercise to make the association between a person's thoughts and his or her feelings. Ask your children what type of feeling would probably happen if a child thought,
"Oh, no—I didn't know there was a math test today."
Feeling_____

"What do you mean I'm grounded?"
Feeling_____

"I'm a worthless person."
Feeling_____

"Life stinks."
Feeling_____

"It's not fair."
Feeling_____

"I found a ten dollar bill as I was walking down the street."
Feeling_____

"My mom and dad are having an argument."
Feeling_____

Once kids understand the connection between thoughts and feelings, it is time to move on.

The Top 5 Ways Anger Messes Up Kids' Lives

There are many ways anger can mess up a kid's life. We're going to look at the big ones.

Embarrassment

Ask your children questions such as,

Have you ever done anything really stupid because

you were angry?

Have you ever called someone a name you wish you could take back?

Have you ever made a complete and total fool of yourself when you've gotten angry?

Explain that when people get really angry, the thinking part of their brains sort of stops working until they can "chill out." That's why people do such stupid stuff when they get mad.

Wasted Time and Energy
Ask your kids this:
What has your anger ever gotten for you?

Has your anger made you any friends?   Yes   No

Has anyone ever paid you to get angry?   Yes No

Has anger helped you meet cute girl/guy? Yes   No

Has anyone ever told you, "I think you're really cool because you get mad all the time?"   Yes No

Has anyone ever given you free pizza because you get angry easily?   Yes No

What has your anger ever gotten you other than into trouble?

We believe anger is usually a waste of time and

energy. It never (or rarely) accomplishes anything positive and it takes a lot of work to stay mad. It wastes the energy you need to live, strive, and survive.

Friendship Problems

Anger also has a way of wrecking kids' friendships. Kids with little patience have a tendency to fly off the handle. It's no fun being around unpredictable people who explode and lose control when they get angry.

Bad Stuff Happens When Kids Get Angry

A lot of bad stuff happens when kids lose their cool and get ticked off because they act without thinking. Their brains don't work right when they get angry. Things get smashed. They say things they can't take back.

Let's not forget, anger leads to a lot of violence.

Anger and Health

There is increasing evidence that people with a lot of anger are headed for serious health problems. Let's examine a couple of experiments that illustrate this point.

First, people with high rates of anger are **four to five times more likely to develop heart disease and one and one-half times more likely to develop cancer.** Learning to handle your anger can be a life saver!

Second, some people still believe that it's good to "get your anger out" by hitting a pillow or something. They still want to "blow off steam" because they believe that it's healthy to "express anger." This is WRONG. Ready for the truth? The body knows **no difference** between anger

72

held in and anger let out. The changes in heart rate and blood pressure are identical. The feelings of anger still cause damage.

Anger-Causing Beliefs

What exact type of thoughts make kids angry? Let's find out.

Have your child look at this list of thoughts and put an "X" after the ones that probably cause anger.

1. "People shouldn't be such idiots."_____
2. "I don't like homework but I guess I can stand it."_____
3. "Even though my parents can be hard to live with, they're not the worst parents in the world."_____
4. "My friends have to listen to what I say. If they don't, they deserve to suffer."_____
5. "My life stinks because people don't do what I tell them to do."_____
6. "This class shouldn't be so hard."_____
7. "I wish my teacher would help me when I'm stuck but I can always ask a friend in study hall for help."_____

If the child put an "X" next to statements 1, 4, 5, and 6, give him or her a pat on the back. These four statements will probably bring about anger because they all do one thing:

THEY DEMAND SOMETHING

The other statements are still "hoping" or "wishing"

something different will happen, but they're not demanding. You've all heard the old saying, "Where there's smoke, there's fire." Replace a few words, and you'll end up with another true statement:

"Where there's a demand, there's anger."

See if your child can make a list of "demanding" words.

If he or she is having a hard time, here are some hints. Look for the "naughty" words that bring about anger. They are:

Should	Can't
Shouldn't	Never
Must	Always
Must not	
Have to	
Ought to	

Ask your kids if they can hear themselves thinking any of those "naughty" words? Any words that are demands will bring about anger.

Body Cues

There are certain things that happen in a person's body right before he or she gets mad. Sometimes people may not be aware when these "body cues" are happening, but it's important that kids learn to recognize them. These cues are like a siren warning people just before they go ballistic. When kids recognize what happens to their bodies before they get angry, they'll have a moment to chill out before they do something really stupid or say something they'll regret later.

Everybody has some kind of body cue that occurs just before they get angry. Here are a few of the more common ones. People say they:
- feel warm all over
- make fists with their hands
- have a clenched jaw and hold their teeth very tight
- start shaking all over
- feel their muscles get tight, especially in their arms

Everybody has a different set of body cues. Have your child think for a moment and then write down what happens in his or her body just before he or she gets mad.

1._____

2._____

3._____

Distraction

The goal of all this is to help kids learn how NOT to become angry when things don't go their way. Handling disappointment is a big part of learning patience. Nobody is lucky enough to go through life without a whole heap of disappointment. The earlier kids learn to handle it, the better.

There are things kids can do while they're learning these skills to keep themselves out of trouble. One of the best is distraction.

It's simple. Kids distract themselves by thinking of something other than the situation they're getting ticked off about. But it's not that easy because when people get mad the ONLY thing they seem to be able to think about is the person or situation that's bugging them. It's sort of like when you're starving, pizza is the only thing on your mind. That's why kids need to decide what to think about BEFORE they start getting angry.

Help your child pick a scene to think about *before* they get ticked off. This memory should be either the happiest or funniest thing you can remember. For example:

- The time he or she hit a home run to win a game.
- The time he or she got the perfect present for Christmas.
- The best birthday party ever.
- A day when it snowed so much school was canceled.

Have your child take a few minutes to think about his or her distraction scene, then write it down below.

_____

_____

_____

_____

_____

It's important that your child has picked a good scene. *Now your child needs to practice imagining this scene several times daily for the next few days.* Have your child use all the details he or she can possibly remember.

What were the people wearing?

What were the sounds around them?

76

Were there any smells in the air?

Try to make the scene just like watching a video.

The idea is for them to switch to this scene when they find themselves getting angry.

THERE IS NO WAY A KID CAN THINK OF HIS OR HER DISTRACTION SCENE AND STILL BECOME ANGRY. It is absolutely impossible. Since anger is produced by thinking demanding thoughts, thinking about a funny or happy memory will keep a child from getting really upset. It will buy the child time to calm down. That few seconds of time could be the difference between handling a situation and blowing it. Sometimes it is better to postpone dealing with an angry situation by using your distraction scene. After distracting yourself, you'll be more in control and able to think and react better.

The Turtle Technique

A technique that can be quite effective with younger children (3 to 7) is known as the Turtle Technique. As the name implies, it is based on a turtle's tendency to curl up into its shell when it becomes upset. You teach the child about turtles and their tendency to close their bodies up when they feel strong emotions coming. Then both of you practice "turtling."

When the child is starting to become upset the adult simply calls the prompt, "It's time to turtle" and the child curls up into his or her imaginary shell. If the child wants to continue to talk or argue simply say, "Turtles never talk when they are in their shell. We can be like turtles and stay quite for awhile when we're upset."

Anger Incident Practice Sheet

Below is a practice sheet to examine any instances in which anger was present. Using practice sheets is a good way to examine the thoughts that lead to anger. You may want to make copies of this sheet to use numerous times when kids lose their temper.

Directions: Complete the practice sheet with as much accuracy as possible. Pretend you are recording this event as if you were a video camera with sound. A video camera couldn't show someone being mean to you. It could show someone calling you names.

1. When did you make yourself angry?
   (What date and time was it?)

2. Where were you when you made yourself angry?

3. Who else was present?

4. As specifically as possible, describe what happened.

5. What did you say to yourself to make yourself angry? (Hint—Listen to your thoughts and see if you can hear any SHOULDS, MUSTS, or OUGHT TO BES)

6. How could you change what you said to yourself to change your feelings? (Hint—Try changing your demanding SHOULDS, etc. to preferences like I WISH..., IT WOULD BE NICE..., I'D LIKE..)

Central Points

1. Helping kids manage their anger is an important step toward self-discipline and patience.

2. It starts with the recognition that anger, like all emotions, is generated by our thoughts and beliefs.

3. Feelings of anger are brought about by demanding thoughts often containing words such as *should, must, have to, always,* and *never.*

4. Helping kids learn their body cues for anger will give them time to distract themselves before losing their cool.

5. The use of a predetermined distraction scene is highly recommended.

9

An ounce of
patience is worth
a pound of brains.
Dutch Proverb

Putting the Plan into Action

We want to thank you for taking the time to read this book. Your commitment of time and energy is to be commended because it's more comfortable to simply turn on the television and ignore problems.

Now we are asking you to do one final thing—turn these ideas into action. It's easy to read a book and learn new ideas with the intention of making change. However, once you get busy at work, and a week or two goes by, the chances for real change become slim. That's why we are challenging you to make an action plan now. Let us help. We've selected a topic that will probably appeal to most readers—improving school work. As we systematically review the ideas in the book, we'll attempt to apply those principles to the issue of improving academic performance. You can certainly select another issue to use for your plan. Let our review serve as a guide.

Backing Up to the Start

Recall the findings of Mischel and his colleagues from the marshmallow studies. More than 600 preschoolers were tested during the initial portion of these experiments. Ten years following the testing, researchers again contacted the families. The adolescents who were able to wait longer (when they were tested as preschoolers) were described by their parents as:

1) More academically competent
2) More socially competent
3) Better at coping with frustration
4) More able to resist temptation
5) More able to cope with stress
6) More verbally fluent
7) More attentive
8) Better planners
9) More able to think ahead
10) More mature

Mischel and his colleagues also found seconds of delay time in preschool were significantly related to scores on the Scholastic Aptitude Test (SAT) later in high school. Children who waited longer (i.e., exhibited more patience) as preschoolers did significantly better on the most commonly used college entrance examination. What does impatience cost? Scholarships!

Patience and LFT

Recall the discussion from chapter 4 regarding patience and Low Frustration Tolerance (LFT). LFT is a common problem in education because schooling involves many frustrating events. It is virtually impossible to be successful in school without having the ability to tolerate at least a moderate amount of frustration.

When the following behaviors are observed, LFT may be a primary or contributing factor:

1) Whining
2) Complaining
3) Day-dreaming
4) Lack of responsibility
5) Withdrawal or shyness

Overcoming LFT

To overcome LFT, start by pointing out the consequences of the children's choices. When kids are grounded for poor school work, trace the problem back to when they originally made a poor decision. It isn't a teacher's fault when students decided not to study for a test.

Where to Begin?

If your goal is to improve school work, start by contacting your child's teachers. **The first, and by far the most important, step is for parents and educators to work together.** Rarely can any significant school problem be corrected without cooperation between home and school.

If you have already been discussing the problem with your child's teacher and things are still not improving, it's time to get together for a face-to-face meeting. Sometimes waiting until regularly scheduled parent-teacher conferences isn't practical.

Once a parent/teacher meeting has been scheduled, it's important for the parents to be clear regarding their objectives. The intent of the meeting which should be 1) to gather and share information, and 2) to start formulating a multi-dimensional plan to get the child back on track.

Questions to Ask

It may be helpful to prepare a list of questions to remind yourself of the points you want to cover during the meeting. Here are some of the suggestions previously mentioned:

1) What seems to be the cause of my child's grade in math? reading? etc.
2) What can I do as a parent to help?
3) When does he/she ask for help in class?
4) When does he/she appear to be paying attention in class? How can this be explained?
5) When does he/she seem to be rushing through his/her work? How can this be explained?
6) When does he/she participate in class discussion?
7) When is his/her work turned in on time?
8) When does my child follow directions?
9) Is the problem with test scores, daily assignments, or both?
10) Is there a need for a follow-up meeting to determine how well the current plan is working?

Reports Home

In order to coordinate communication between home and school, it is recommended that some type of routine report be sent home to parents. When school and parents keep in close contact, many of the avenues that students use to avoid work are simply no longer available. Communication is a key ingredient to make certain problem with impatience don't become established as a pattern.

Homework

It's a good idea to have a prearranged location and time for homework. Check frequently to make certain the child is on task. Some kids will need more reminders to stay focused. These reminders can take different shapes and don't have to be delivered in a nagging tone. It's also a good idea to break up assignments into manageable chunks.

Teaching Kids the Skill of Using Patient Self-Talk

Self-Instructional Training (SIT), discussed in chapter 6, is a four step process that requires the help and guidance of an adult. **Step One** - The adult does a math problem while talking aloud to himself or herself about the strategy to use. For example, the adult may be saying something such as:

> "I have to go slow to get it right.
> I'll make certain I look at
> the sign so I don't do the wrong

work. It's a plus sign so I'll be adding. Okay, four plus nine is more than 10. I borrow one from the four, add it to nine and I have 10. Now I only have to add the three left to ten and I have the answer, 13. Once you get to the number 10, it's easy. I'm going very slow and being careful. I'm doing a good job."

It's also a good idea to intentionally make a mistake and model how to cope with that.

"Four plus nine is 11. Oops. That's not the right answer. I made a mistake because I didn't go slow and think about my answer. That's okay. I'll be sure to get the right answer this time."

Step 2 - Let the child use the pencil now to do a similar addition problem. The adult is to talk aloud guiding the child's work. The same type of verbalizations are to be used. Praise the child for following your lead and doing the math correctly.

Step 3 - Now let the child practice on a similar math problem, but instead of the adult talking the child through it, tell the child to talk (aloud) to himself or herself while working on the problem. The adult should remind the child to "go slow" and "check all the way before you write down an answer." Praise the child for using self-talk and for exhibiting patience on the problem.

Let kids practice several problems this way until they get used to talking aloud while they work. Do as many problems as you feel is necessary before proceeding.

Step 4 - Now it's time for the child to do the math problem while talking silently to himself or herself. Just as before, remind the child to "go slow" and "be careful." This time their verbalizations are only in their head.

Teaching Self-Evaluation

It's a good idea to evaluate your action plan on a regular basis. Appraisal is a central feature to any major endeavor. A child's education is far too important not to evaluate his or her progress at regular intervals of time.

As has been stressed throughout the book, don't think that a child can change a long-held pattern of behavior in a week or two. It takes time and consistent effort. Don't be discouraged if you haven't seen a complete turn around in a short period of time.

The child should be a part of this evaluation. Start by asking her, "How do you think you've been doing with the things we've been doing to make school go better?" It's important for kids to learn the skill of self-evaluation. Such a talent will serve her well throughout life.

In this case, self-evaluation is even more important because to appraise your performance, you must first be able to *reflect* on your behavior. Patience and reflection go hand in hand. It's very hard to accomplish one without having the other.

If the child believes school is going better, ask her,

"In what way is school going better?" This will force her to carefully examine exactly what she's doing for the change to occur. If she's correct and her school work is improving, praise her not only for her effort, but also for her ability to identify what she's doing to turn things around.

If school isn't improving, redouble your efforts. Consider the following:

Do you need to speak to the teacher again?

Where is your plan breaking down?

What obstacles weren't accounted for?

How can those obstacles be overcome (or worked around)?

Are there any areas of school that are improving?

What is different about those situations?

Final Thoughts

In the final analysis, it all comes back to you, the reader. Consider that good news because left to their own devices, children do a lousy job of raising themselves. By their nature, they often make poor decisions that are not in their best interests.

We have one final challenge for you. As an adult, you need to have the patience to persevere until the child has learned these important skills. Children can't do it alone. They are looking to us for assistance. Let's not miss this opportunity to do the right thing and teach children how to live a patient, and happier, life.

If we can be of assistance to you on this journey, don't hesitate to contact us at jwilde@indiana.edu.

Notes

Chapter 1: Introduction

1. V. Fuchs (1988) *Women's Quest for Economic Equality*, Cambridge, MA: Harvard University Press, p. 111.

2. N. Gibbs (1989) "How America has Run Out of Time," *Time*, April 24, p. 59.

3. S. Tifft (1989) "A Crisis Looms in Science," *Time*, September 11, p. 68.

4. G. Duncan and S. Hoffman (1985) "A Reconsideration of the Economic Consequences of Marital Dissolution," *Demography*, 22, 4, p. 485 - 497.

5. L. Robins, J. Helzer, M. Weismann, H. Orvaschel, E. Gruenberg, J. Burke, and D. Reiger (1984) "Lifetime Prevalence of Psychiatric Disorders in Three Sites," *Archives of General Psychiatry*, 41, p. 949 - 958.

6. Center for Disease Control (1991) "Attempted Suicide Among High School Students-United States, 1990," *Morbidity and Mortality Weekly Report*, p. 633.

7.   J. Wilde (1994) "The Effects of the Let's Get Rational Board Game on Rational Thinking, Depression and Self-Acceptance in Adolescents," *The Journal of Rational-Emotive and Cognitive Behavior Therapy*, 12, 3, p. 189 - 196.

8.   L. Johnston, J. Bachman, and P. O'Malley (1995) "Monitoring the Future," Available http://www.pitt.edu/~cedar.html

Chapter 2: Why is Patience Important?

1.   W. Mischel, Y. Shoda, and P. Peake (1988) "The Nature of Adolescent Competencies Predicted by Preschool Delay of Gratification," *Journal of Personality and Social Psychology*, 54, p. 687 - 696.

2.   B. Yates and W. Mischel (1979) "Young Children's Preferred Attentional Strategies and Delaying Gratification," *Journal of Personality and Social Psychology*, 37, p. 286 - 300.

3.   H. N. Mischel and W. Mischel (1983) "The Development of Children's Knowledge of Self-Control Strategies," *Child Development*, 54, p. 603 - 619.

4.   W. Mischel, E. Ebbesen, and A. Zeiss (1972) "Cognitive and Attentional Mechanisms in Delay of Gratification," *Journal of Personality and Social*

Psychology, 2, p. 204 - 218.

5.   W. Mischel and B. Moore (1980) "The Role of
      Ideation in Voluntary Delay for Symbolically
      Presented Rewards," *Cognitive Therapy and Research*,
      4, p. 211 - 221.

6.   M. Nisan and A. Koriat (1984) "The Effect of
      Cognitive Restructuring on Delay of Gratification,"
      Child Development, 55, p. 492 - 503.

7.   Y. Shoda, W. Mischel, and P. Peake (1990)
      "Predicting Adolescent Cognitive and Self-
      Regulatory Competencies From Preschool Delay of
      Gratification: Identifying Diagnostic Conditions,"
      Developmental Psychology, 26, p. 978 - 986.

Chapter 3: The Attention-Deficit Hyperactivity Disorder Explosion

1.   F. Baughman (1999) "The ADHD Consensus
      Conference: End of the Epidemic." *The Brown
      University Child and Adolescent Behavior Letter*,
      15, p. 8.

Chapter 4: Patience and Low Frustration Tolerance

1. W. Knaus (1974) *Rational-Emotive Education: A Manual for Elementary School Teachers*. New York, Institute for Rational-Emotive Therapy.

2. J. Bard and H. Fischer (1983) "A Rational-Emotive Approach to Underachievement." In Ellis and Bernard (Eds.) *Rational-Emotive Approaches to the Problems of Childhood*. New York, Plenium Press.

Chapter 5: The Consequences of Impatience

1. L. Otto, V. Call, and K. Spenner (1981) *Design for a Study of Entry into Careers*. Lexington, MA: Lexington.

2. R. McCloskey, C. Evahn, and L. Kratzer (1992) *High School Underachievers: What do They Achieve as Adults?* Newbury Park, CA: Sage.

Chapter 6: Teaching Children to Talk to Themselves

1. L. S. Vygotsky (1962) *Thought and Language*. Wiley and Sons, New York.

2. A. R. Luria (1973) *The Working Brain*, Penguin Books, New York.

3. D. Meichenbaum and J. Goodman (1971) "Training

Impulsive Children to Talk to Themselves: A Means of Developing Self-Control," *Journal of Abnormal Psychology*, *77*, p. 115 - 126.

About the Authors

Jerry Wilde is an assistant professor of educational psychology at Indiana University East. He has extensive experience working with children who have learning, emotional and behavioral problems. Dr. Wilde is known for his presentations on topics such as anger management, managing difficult behaviors, and cognitive-behavior therapy.

Polly Wilde has over a decade of experience as a professional writer and currently works as a freelance reporter. She has been the managing editor of a newspaper and was also honored by the National Newspaper Association for her work as a features writer.

Index